Advance Praise for *Do IT Right*

Marty has been my most trusted source, not just for the technology side of business, but business in general. He is a true strategic thinker.

—MIKE DELEHANTY, EXECUTIVE VICE
PRESIDENT, MOUNTAIN WEST FINANCIAL

Marty has taken what was a necessary evil and transformed it into a necessary component of our strategic growth and profitability.

—PATRICK SOMERS, GENERAL MANAGER, GENERAL
AIR CONDITIONING AND PLUMBING

Bringing on Marty and his team was one of the best decisions we've ever made. He is a visionary and has the unique ability to integrate information technology with the operational needs of an organization.

—TRACY THOMAS, CHIEF FINANCIAL OFFICER,
NATIONAL COMMUNITY RENAISSANCE

Marty and his team really are superheroes in the increasingly complex world of IT. I love recommending Marty to my clients.

—GARY LOCKWOOD, CHAIR, VISTAGE INTERNATIONAL

Marty and his team take great care in staying at the cutting edge of information technology for all types of business needs, both big and small.

—KIRK R. HOWIE, ASSISTANT GENERAL MANAGER-ADMINISTRATION, THREE VALLEYS MUNICIPAL WATER DISTRICT

Marty's team took IT off the table of concerns we had and let us focus on our industry and business goals.

—MIKE POMA, CEO, POMA DISTRIBUTING COMPANY, INC.

Marty and Accent have provided the technological expertise for our financial services firm to fully implement and embrace technology, saving us time and expense—while exceeding regulatory and security hurdles.

—KERRICK W. BUBB, M.B.A., AIF®, PRESIDENT, KWB WEALTH MANAGERS GROUP

Do **IT** Right

Do IT Right

It's Not About The Computers

MARTY KAUFMAN

ISBN   978-1-61961-461-1   *Paperback*

978-1-61961-462-8   *Ebook*

LIONCREST

PUBLISHING

Contents

1. The IT Problem 9

2. Why We Think IT Is Evil......................... 31

3. How to Mismanage Your IT 51

4. Get the Most From Your IT...................... 71

5. From Problem to Strategic Asset.............. 89

6. The IT Solution 109

About the Author 127

Over the course of reading this book, you may find your-self with questions. I would love to have the opportunity to answer questions or communicate with you regarding your Information Technology or Business Growth challenges. Just send an email to MartyK@TeamAccent.com and I will be happy to respond.

Thanks,
Marty

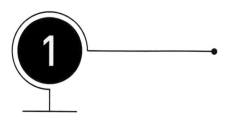

The IT Problem

For most businesses, information technology (IT) just doesn't compute. The problem is most people don't really know what IT is or how to manage the function effectively. I have been in the IT business as an employee and a business owner for about thirty years. About fifteen years ago, it really hit me. I had to ask myself, "Why does it seem like us IT guys are letting our bosses and/or customers down? Why is it that no matter how hard we try, there always seems to be more expected of us?" After contemplating this dilemma for quite a long time, it came to me. I knew that I did not know it all and that I never would. I knew that there was so much to be learned and that no one person could handle "all" of the IT function effectively. It was then that I realized my desire to help business leaders and owners get the most from the investment they are making in IT.

If you're a company president, a business owner, or a CEO in a company of fifteen to five hundred employees, you probably have an information technology problem. The worst part is, you may not even know it.

At the heart of any successful business is return on investment. When it comes to IT, however, few C-level executives know if they're getting good value on the money they invest. They don't know if they're getting good results, let alone the *best possible* results.

In the real world of business, markets, and stiff competition, IT isn't just hardware and software, computers and networks. It's the people behind the scenes, the management of those people, and the information that flows under their fingertips.

Unfortunately, there's a lot of misinformation out there about IT. People see technology management as too technical and intimidating, so most of the time they just ignore the issues or resort to the infamous "just handle it" approach. In the business world, that's when problems start, and they get worse by the day. Misinformation leads to mismanagement, which brings us to the core of the problem.

Doing IT Wrong: A Few Examples

Take, for example, the law firm that contacted me with a request for a quote (RFQ) to consult on their IT. They already had an IT guy on staff who'd been there for quite a while.

They'd sent their RFQ to several companies like mine and no others had responded. I called them out of courtesy to explain why I wouldn't be responding to their RFQ with a quote. "Why not?" the practice administrator asked me. She was genuinely perplexed. She'd had no responses to her RFQ from any other IT consultants. I explained that she had sent out an RFQ more suited to a company of thousands, if not hundreds of thousands of employees, as if her small law firm were General Motors. Even a consulting firm like mine with over fifty IT specialists would have trouble meeting the specifications of the majority of the RFQ.

I met with the practice administrator and managing partner who basically presented a laundry list of IT responsibilities they'd cut and pasted from a website. They were a forty-person firm that had stumbled on an IT blueprint for a Fortune 1000 company!

It wasn't their fault; they just didn't know better. They were expecting their IT guy to fill the multiple roles of a practice consultant, a programmer, an IT help desk, a security administrator, a systems analyst, a chief information officer, and that was just for starters. It wasn't humanly possible.

I went through a description of all the roles they expected one individual to fill. I explained that there are many disciplines involved in IT, from programmers to information technology architects, and each of those people has highly specialized skills.

On another occasion, I was contacted by a small manufacturing firm with about sixty desktop-computer users. I met with the chief financial officer (CFO) who told me they had an IT person on staff, but they were dissatisfied with that person's performance. He told me that his IT guy was basically picking and choosing the tasks that suited him. "He doesn't do the stuff we need to get done. He claims he does what's necessary, but we're not sure what that is," said the CFO. "We don't even know if he's doing a good job or not. It's like he is holding us hostage."

I asked, "What is it that you want him to do?" He told me, "Well, we want him to manage our ERP [enterprise resource planning system], our CRM [customer relationship management], we need him to answer end-user questions whenever they come up, keep us secure, be the IT Manager, etc." They also wanted him to research business processes for them. It was a tall order, and the fact is that one person couldn't do it all.

A larger company contacted me with a different kind of problem. This company employed four hundred people in real estate using a broad range of information technology in locations all over the United States. They had their own full-scale IT department. Over the course of two years, I was called in three times to discuss their technology performance. They'd gone through multiple IT managers, help-desk people, administrators, and systems analysts, and they couldn't understand why the results were so poor or why they had so much employee turnover.

"We have a real problem," they told me. "IT has become an excuse staff members use to not get their jobs done!" *IT as an excuse*. This is a phrase that I quote time and time again now.

I found that their IT problem extended through every department and level of the organization, including management, primarily because there was no accountability for IT. No one in management or among IT staff had the experience or know-how to manage IT functions across the company. The result was that the company's productivity suffered and some potentially good IT people were replaced.

Sound Familiar?

Perhaps you recognize your own company's IT problem in these stories. Or perhaps you're at an earlier stage of growing a company and you want to avoid the common pitfalls of IT. As my book title suggests, you want to find a way to *Do IT Right*.

During my thirty years as an IT consultant, I've worked with thousands of companies, many in dire straits with their IT. Of course each company is unique, but the similarities among companies are striking. In many cases the fixes are similar, too. But before we get to all that, I have a few more examples to show you that are very revealing. They also may be quite familiar.

I was called in by a warehouse-management consultant to evaluate whether a company's information technology would allow them to install an automated warehouse-management system. I met with all the players individually, including the owner, the IT manager, and the warehouse manager. I asked the owner if his staff, who are the end users of IT, were happy. He told me, "They're always complaining about email, documents and spreadsheets, and our systems and processes." But when I spoke to the IT manager, he told me everyone had exactly what they needed.

So I met with staff members directly. They described their full range of problems, which, it turned out, had something in common. They told me that the IT manager was hard to work with, but the owner wasn't aware of it. The IT manager may have been smart, but nobody liked him, so they would suffer through problems instead of asking for the help they so desperately needed.

When it comes to IT, personalities can play as big a role as information technology itself in getting things right or getting them wrong. As you'll see in this book, best practices in IT management are similar to best practices in business management generally.

For example, a mortgage company I worked with had more than three hundred people on staff and a full IT department. Their nagging problem was that their IT systems weren't reliable and so the productivity of the employees was way down. Updates weren't done on time, the system was not available during business hours, backups weren't working, and end users weren't happy.

My specialists went in and did analyses, updates, and upgrades for them. They had somewhere in the neighborhood of eighty file servers, which is a lot. Things got better, for a while. They had a lot of the right folks in place: an IT manager, help-desk people, and systems analysts, but they weren't getting the results they wanted. Where things broke down was in their day-to-day management of the system and the department.

When I asked, "On a daily basis, who does this specific task?" they said, "Well, nobody." What they lacked was someone to manage and administer the back end of their IT department.

What's the back end? Picture a room with firewalls, Web filters, switches, routers, virtualized servers, operating systems, and lots and lots of cables and equipment. You could think of it as the "guts" of IT—the parts most users never see. Somebody has to manage and administer all of this stuff, keeping it up to date and tuned up. But in this case, nobody had the specific responsibility to do the job.

Common Problems and Mistakes

Are you recognizing a pattern? Frequently the management team responsible for the IT team doesn't know what's really going on. They don't know the possibilities. They don't know their options. CEOs don't know how to get better results.

The bottom line is that most companies don't know how to *think* about IT. They don't even know enough to know what they don't know. And it isn't their fault. Information technology is so broad and so specialized that it's hard for management to get a handle on it.

Even when things are humming along fine, how do you know it's the best you can get? Could your systems work better? People tend not to look into things when they appear to be going well—they wait until a problem arises, and it usually does.

For very small start-ups, information technology isn't all that complicated. At the very early stage it's enough to have computers and software, email, Google Docs, Cloud storage, and a WordPress website. You don't need expensive firewalls for security, yet. It's all doable up to a point. However, when you get to thirty, one hundred, or more people on staff, things begin to get complicated. Document management alone can become a problem. With everyone storing data in the Cloud with different vendors, how do you know where your company data is? When you reach this level of complexity with desktops and mobile devices, you need a lot more than just a number to call for help.

As companies grow, so do their IT needs, and so do their questions:

- Is everything secure?
- Are we safe from Internet threats?
- What would happen in case of a disaster? Would we be able to recover all of our information?
- What would happen if the IT person or people quit?
- Are we getting the most for our money from our IT?

These are the kinds of questions that keep CEOs awake at night. What happens is that the CEO, the business owner, the company president, or manager is gradually set up for disappointment. They hire a family member or friend who seems to be good with computers and assume all will be taken care of. But over time, as the company grows, there's a slow realization that their information technology is falling short. No one seems to know which pieces go where.

Business owners have many skills. They do many jobs inside their organizations. When they're starting out, entrepreneurs frequently do their own accounting, fundraising, and marketing. They even learn to plug in their own computers and get them working on the Internet. But as they grow they tend to be clueless about what it takes to keep their businesses secure, compliant, backed up, and prepared to recover in the event of a disaster.

On a day-to-day basis managers and owners typically

don't know how to manage their IT. They don't know what they should be measuring. They don't know the metrics for IT. And to their detriment, they don't realize that the friend they put in charge of IT can't handle it all.

And importantly, they haven't put a strategy in place for in-house technology goals and objectives. They don't know how to optimize their IT.

Marketing Is Not IT

A common mistake that trips up some companies is confusing marketing with IT. When a growing company assigns their Web developer to handle IT, it's the beginning of trouble.

Marketing, by its nature, is a creative function. It isn't a technical function. Yes, graphic designers create ads and other marketing material using computer software. Yes, marketers depend on social media such as Facebook and Twitter to reach potential customers.

But for marketing people, computer systems are tools that help them do their jobs. That's as far as it goes for them. You may find someone who is tech savvy and can make their way around technology, but they are not the right people to fix, manage, and administer an IT department.

IT is a different skill set altogether. Asking a marketer to handle IT is like asking a driver to design and build his own car.

IT Isn't Like Baseball—or Maybe It Is

In a similar way, asking one person who fancies technology to cover the entire field of IT with all its specialization is like asking a pitcher to cover all the bases, as well as the outfield—and, while he's at it, to manage the team. In a company with thirty to three hundred people, not only is the job too vast, but each component requires different skills. Pitchers aren't catchers.

Different functions in IT also attract different personality types. Systems analysts and software engineers don't typically have the people skills of help-desk troubleshooters. Remember, IT isn't just about computers; it's about people. Unlike baseball caps, IT is not "one size fits all."

When it comes to information technology, company managers may also find themselves on the wrong field or even out of their league. They know how to determine whether the accounts payable and accounts receivable departments are performing well. They know how to measure the effectiveness of their cost-accounting group. But IT is a different game. When problems develop off the field, in the tall grass, management just isn't prepared. They don't know how or where to look.

I mentioned earlier that managers don't know the metrics for measuring IT performance. At the help-desk level, for instance, they need to account for how many end-user problems are resolved in a day or an hour. What's a good measure of that? How would anyone know?

At the level of network operations, how do you know if the job is getting done? Network-operations people work on firewalls and antivirus software. They automate the prevention of inbound threats and outbound situations. They monitor disaster-recovery programs and keep the corporate environment protected. How can you be sure that they know exactly what they need to know to do their jobs effectively?

Let's say your staff uses upwards of thirty or more desktop PCs. Are every one of those machines secure? Are your firewalls protecting from threats? Are your backups restorable? How would you know?

That IT guy you hired two years ago may be a very personable and skilled troubleshooter, but try to send him in to handle network operations, and he'll be lost in the weeds for a year. He's a great catcher and a good base runner, but he doesn't play at that level.

Ideally, the player you'd have in that management position is your chief information officer (CIO). This is the person who can see the entire field from a high level. He knows exactly what the help-desk people are up to and what network operations is doing. He interacts with those human beings on the other side of the keyboards and asks, "Is there anything getting in the way of your doing your job?"

At an even higher level, way up in the skyboxes where the air is thin, are your IT architects. When the CEO asks, "What will it take for our IT to handle an expansion of fifty or a hundred more people?" the architect enters the field. He puts together the specs and the IT framework and infrastructure to make expansion possible. It may involve virtualization, storage, network communications, Cloud systems, on-site file servers—whatever it takes. The architect works out the solutions.

You see what I'm driving at? IT staffing depends on the size of an organization and the complexities that go with it. And at the same time, IT plays a vital role in business planning. Problems arise when company management sends a pitcher to the mound and expects to win the game without surveying the field or hiring the key players who can help make it happen. It's all a matter of technology management, which we'll get into more deeply in Chapter 4.

Are You Flying by the Seat of Your Pants?

Information technology is a problem for many businesses because management inadvertently lets it become a problem. Most everyone has taken a trip on an airplane. We all expect the airlines to perform the necessary daily, hourly, and yearly maintenance that it takes to keep us safe while airborne. How comfortable would you feel as an airline passenger if you knew that the plane you had just boarded had not been maintained at all? I know I don't want to fly on a plane that has not had current maintenance, and I am sure most people would agree with me. Unfortunately, this is how many businesses approach IT: without routine care and upkeep.

Every organization, even those of fewer than thirty desktop users, needs to take IT seriously. It's a fact of life that to succeed in business today companies need to know how to make IT more than just "running"; IT needs to be a strategic asset.

IT isn't simply about the help desk and fixing immediate technical problems. It's about getting real business results. And for anyone who follows the news, it's about security. You should be no more likely to leave your business unprotected than to leave your car unlocked in a parking lot.

And speaking of parking lots, I have a perfect example.

My client in this situation was an apartment complex complete with a health club and garage. Parking was set up with an access-control system activated by car-key fobs to open the gates. The problem was that the entire system, including the gym, was connected to the same network. If a single one of the Internet-connected treadmills malfunctioned, the whole system was affected and no one could access the garage or get into the complex! Talk about some unhappy tenants! The parallel here is that the end users of the company IT system should not find themselves locked out of their business systems because of lack of maintenance and management.

All business owners want their employees working. They don't want technology to get in the way. They don't want downtime. It's a productivity issue. Information technology is an investment in productivity, as well as security.

When IT is done right, it provides an excellent return on investment (ROI). That's the goal. How do you get the best results and the best return? In competitive markets it's about getting ahead of the curve and besting the competition. And the way to get there is to have your IT functioning optimally and providing you a competitive advantage.

The Expectations Problem

CEOs and business leaders generally haven't taken a course in college called "How to get the most from your IT department." So when it comes to managing IT, it's easy to get tripped up and tangled in a whole bunch of impossible expectations.

From the point of view of a general manager or operations manager, an IT person is the guy to call when something doesn't work. Meanwhile, the IT guy is busy doing what he thinks he should do. He's trying to cover all the bases, but many times he's working on projects that might not be the most important to the organization overall.

At my company, we hire on the basis of workplace personality tests to help ensure we hire the right people for the right positions. We use the Core Values Index (CVI) developed by Taylor Protocols. In these tests, people generally fall into one of four categories: builder, merchant, banker, or innovator. As we've already seen, there are many disciplines in IT, and they are suited to different personality types. A programmer will either be a builder or an innovator; she will almost never be a merchant. Merchant personalities who like to communicate with others are best suited to the help desk or the position of chief information officer (CIO) at the executive level. (For more on workplace personality testing, see Chapter 2.)

The IT guy who is working solo has to wear many hats. He feels overextended, so he naturally gravitates to what he likes best. In many cases he's a builder or an innovator type of person. So when he's had his fill of helping end users and is tired of crawling under desks, he lobbies for a new hire to do the menial tasks. The small empire building begins. He also lobbies for a budget to build systems that will last several years, and when they're built, he maintains them for a while and is bored again. What he really wants to do is manage the network or build new stuff. The only problem is the entire system is usually too small to really require a dedicated network manager and a system architect.

But does the general manager know that? Not very likely. So he goes along with the plan. His expectations are that everything will be covered and operate efficiently.

I see this all the time in my consulting. Organizations of thirty, one hundred, three hundred, or more desktop users fall into a trap of misguided expectations. Management expects that, day or night, weekend or holidays, their IT guy will be there. If there's a problem tomorrow, he'll be there. If he's got to fly back from his vacation in Bermuda, he'll be there. The company has backed itself into a corner with their IT, and the problem is they don't know it—yet.

On one occasion I received a call from a tool company

that said, "We have a problem. We need to talk about our IT manager; we're not sure if we can trust him." At our meeting they explained, "We think he's just putting Band-Aids on things. He likes to tinker, likes to do things his own way." They used the same phrase I related earlier in another story: "He's holding us hostage." I hear it all the time.

"What do you mean?" I asked them, but I already knew the answer.

"Well, he's created some stuff around here that he thinks is proprietary, that no one else can touch. And he wants more money for it. He doesn't seem to have our best interests in mind."

We had a long conversation about expectations. What should the guy be doing? What does the company need? Are they getting what they need?

It turns out they weren't getting even the minimum when it came to customer service or help for their own end users. "He doesn't want to help anyone," they said. "He doesn't like them, and they don't like him. They don't think he fixes anything." Finally, they told me, "We're afraid that if we let him go, we'll lose our competitive advantage. We don't want to risk that."

They certainly did need some help. It's a common problem of neglecting to define expectations. Managers are left not knowing what to expect. They don't have business practices in place to manage their IT.

Management Principles for IT

CEOs don't intentionally ignore IT. They just don't have a reasonable idea of what to do from a management perspective. You need to be sure that your company's IT is delivering appropriate expectations daily, weekly, monthly, yearly, and into the future. You need to apply sound management principles, measurable metrics, and service levels to IT as you would to your operations, accounting, sales, or any other department.

Business leaders need to learn how to manage their company's IT for every stage of growth. In most situations it means knowing how to assemble a team and put the right people in place. IT should be treated like any other department or division in your organization. It requires oversight and planning, established processes and accountability.

Applying management principles to IT means putting in place the kind of reporting and benchmarking that informs your decision-making. When you do that, you'll know what to expect. And what you can expect is the best return on your investment.

IT is a crucial part of your business strategy. If it isn't, you've got a problem. So we'll be taking a good, hard look at principles of management for IT in Chapter 4.

Do IT Right Now

I wrote this book because I want you to *Do IT Right*. I'm passionate about what I do, and I want to share what I know. As a consultant, I do IT every day for my business clients. They have real problems that require intervention. And in the new world of interconnectivity with ever-increasing mobile technologies, IT problems are only getting worse. They are more complicated and more costly than ever before.

On these pages you'll come to understand the problems, the strategies, and the solutions. I want you to know your options for effectively using IT to grow your business and earn your market share. You don't need any specialized knowledge or training. You don't have to become a computer geek to get the most out of information technology.

Like any business leader, you want to maximize your competitive advantage. For twenty-first-century businesses, information technology is indispensable to achieving success in the marketplace. IT can provide the competitive advantage you're looking for. When you *Do IT Right*, you're better positioned to outperform your competition.

Like my clients, you want to make the right choices for your company's IT. You shouldn't be spending your time and money playing catch-up. You want to be effectively managing your IT and planning ahead.

I want you to get the kind of results Fortune 1000 companies get from their IT, but at an affordable cost. The fact is that when IT is done right, it actually costs less.

You picked up or downloaded this book because you've got an IT problem or you want to optimize your IT. You're serious about success and you want to *Do IT Right* now. The good news is you've already started.

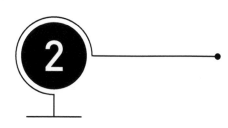

Why We Think IT Is Evil

Why does IT have such a bad rap? Why do people tend to think of information technology as a "necessary evil"?

Typically, business leaders are frustrated and confused by the technical aspects of information technology. IT is one of the few areas of knowledge related to business that business people feel ill-equipped to handle. IT frustrates them.

The average CEO has a working knowledge of budgeting, marketing, sales, accounting, margins, revenue streams, and a whole lot more. When it comes to IT, however, he doesn't know how things work, but he knows he needs it. He needs control of the Internet and software, email and word processing, business applications, order entry, inventory and shop floor. He knows his work orders won't go out without some kind of tracking system. So he hires an IT person to take care of it all.

From the CEO's point of view, IT people are kind of flaky. They speak in technical jargon that most business people don't understand. It's as if, when you ask them what time it is, they'll explain to you how to build a clock. When a CEO or business manager asks, "Why did the system go so slow today?" the IT person starts spouting a bunch of technical terms. The conversation ends with the CEO saying, "Just make it work," and leaving to go do something else.

Information technology is not intuitive for laypeople. A simple electrical fluctuation in a system can make something go wrong at the desktop level. Especially today where speeds are higher and temperatures hotter, end users can experience technical glitches in something as basic as word processing. The screens we look at have millions and millions of things going on behind the scenes. It can even be hard for an expert to get to the root of an end user's problem. So it's understandable why people often feel that IT is evil.

When a business start-up reaches a critical mass of more than thirty end users, the company's IT starts to get really complex. It can take a village to figure out and manage some of the more involved aspects of IT security, networks, and systems. It's frustrating to an owner because it's foreign to him and he doesn't really want to have to deal with it. The common statement I hear from business owners about IT is "I just want it to work." The problem for them is they don't know how to make it work, and to make matters worse, they're not particularly interested in figuring it out.

The Big, Bad "IT" in the Room

For the most part, entrepreneurial folks are not technologically inclined. They have great business minds. They are people with great ideas and energy. They are movers and shakers, take-charge people who are confident with what they know. They have excellent business heads and instincts. But when it comes to IT, they are generally at a loss for how to get the most out of the department.

Information technology is the big "it" in the room that makes them feel extremely uncomfortable. They are put in the awkward position of depending on another person's expertise while not feeling equipped to evaluate that person's work. IT shakes the CEO's confidence. The usual checks and balances normally used to manage don't seem to apply.

From the outset, business owners don't know how to buy IT. Once they have it, they don't know how to manage it. Unlike other departments and areas of their business, they don't know how to make their IT people accountable. As mentioned in Chapter 1, they don't know what metrics to put in place to evaluate whether or not their IT is being handled as it should be.

For example, a business owner knows how to measure the work of the accounting department. He knows that when a bill comes in, it's going to have a due date, and someone in accounting needs to pay that bill on time. If it isn't paid on time, he'll be dealing with the bill again later on. It's a very simple check-and-balance process. If finances aren't done correctly, monthly financial statements will reflect the deficiencies.

When it comes to IT, however, management most likely does not have a clue. The only time they talk with IT staff is when they want to do something new or when something doesn't work. Then the IT guy tells them, "Well, we'll have to buy this and have to build that."

Take the case of a business that wants to add a customer-relationship management system (CRM). The CEO wants to improve the management of customer data and amp up sales and marketing efforts to service customers better. The first response from the technology folks is "We're going to need the Cloud, or we'll have to buy a server and software and get some estimates on that. We'll also need to upgrade disk space because we're filling up our disks right now with everyone's documents. If we install CRM, our data will grow even more."

Already the CEO's eyes are rolling back in his head. He doesn't know whether any or all of that is true. He just wants to improve the customer-business relationship. Now IT is talking about a $50,000 to $100,000 investment. Should he believe his IT guy? He doesn't know.

Most businesses don't have a forward-looking plan for their information technology. They don't know where they're going with IT or how to get there. At the same time, most IT people are focused on the day-to-day interruptions and are most likely not planning either. Seldom do management and IT put their heads together to plan the next strategic step that could make a great impact on business performance and growth.

What Does That IT Guy Have Up His Sleeve?

Technical guys like to diagnose, build, and fix things. This is the basic DNA of most IT technicians. They've been trained as network and computer-systems engineers. They tend to prefer to work independently and often aren't good communicators. Their minds are fixed on a technical track. That is just how they are wired.

Technical people get a bad rap because what they know how to do is mysterious to other people. They know how to build things, make them go faster, increase performance. What they generally don't know is how to communicate effectively with nontechnical people and business leaders.

So when the owner sits down with her IT guy, the conversation usually does not go well. While the boss goes on and on about planning, the IT person's mind is tinkering with the system. He's thinking about the next thing he wants to build. He knows that the new Cloud technology the boss is asking about won't require building on his part. He knows that if they buy and install new file servers, once he puts them in, they'll last as many as eight years. What will he do in the meantime?

If you have a business of thirty to several hundred people, and you only need to build something new every five to eight years, that IT geek loses interest. He doesn't get his kicks from helping staff with their Microsoft Excel and email problems. As I mentioned in Chapter 1, there are many disciplines in IT that tend toward different personality types. Some are more machine-oriented, such as IT engineers, and some are more people-oriented, such as the help-desk person and the CIO. It's very difficult and rare to find all the skills and inclinations in one IT person.

For example, systems analysts, programmers, and Web developers all play a part in information technology. A systems analyst documents the various components of IT in order to develop efficiencies. If a company were developing a new customer-relationship management system, a systems analyst would go around and figure out all the processes that are involved, and then turn it over to a programmer. The programmer would write the software, and then a Web developer would do the Web interface for the Internet.

Web developers and programmers tend to be different sorts of people. Web developers can be very graphics-oriented, whereas programmers are very much the opposite: they're all about data and code.

Yet, business managers are inclined to view all IT people the same. They think "they're really good with computers so..." They majority of the business community thinks that one person should be able to do all the jobs that comprise IT.

In my line of work, which is IT consulting, I hire top-flight

IT specialists in specific disciplines. When I send out an individual or team to bring a client's company up to speed, I need to know I've chosen the right people for specific jobs. In order to make the right hire, I put prospective employees through a series of tests.

I test them to see if they're smart, and I test to see if they're team players. I need to know if they are problem solvers and how they are likely to perform in stressful situations. I test specifically for the four personality types mentioned in Chapter 1:

- Builder
- Innovator
- Merchant
- Banker

I need to know if a person is a builder who likes to tinker on his own. Perhaps he's a merchant type, and therefore more of a visionary with people skills who likes to interact with others. Others are innovator types, kind of like scientists who'll sit in a room and think of a dozen ways to solve a problem. I also look for potential hires who have a distinct numbers focus, like a banker. My team has to be strong and cover all areas. Organizations need all four types and literally can't survive if they are missing even one of the basic personality types.

This is where CEOs of small companies miss the mark when it comes to hiring their IT manager. They forget that, along with technical skills, an IT person working solo needs to have the skills necessary to engage in some planning with management. He also needs to feel some degree of comfort in genuine social interactions in order to help staff with their software, hardware, and system problems. If none of the end users will ask for help because the IT manager does not work well with people, the company is no better off.

It's hard to find a person who is all four personality types. However, there are some who overlap. If the four personality types are pictured as four quadrants on a page, such a person would fall somewhere at the center of a box that extends into all four quadrants. She'd be part builder, part merchant, part innovator, and part banker. She'd be a utility player who would be able to get a lot of things done and not be frustrated by any one of them. This person would be good to work with, but still could not possibly be capable of knowing all there is to know about the IT field.

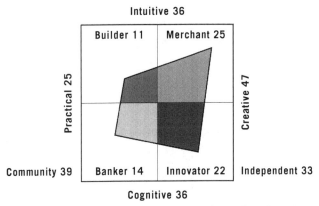

Intuitive 36

Builder 11	Merchant 25
Banker 14	Innovator 22

Practical 25

Creative 47

Community 39

Independent 33

Cognitive 36

Taylor Protocols Inc.

If you look at the way a construction company is organized, you have estimators who look at the money side like bankers, a merchant type who can sell the project, an architect who is an innovator, a builder who can follow the blueprint, a foreman who can oversee the construction team and subcontractors, and skilled labor who actually get the job done in real space.

Unfortunately, because of the masses of information to be known and the technical personality type that IT people usually have, my business clients have usually reached a pretty high level of frustration with their IT by the time they call for consultation. The smaller companies have hired one IT person. Larger firms either have an internal team or have outsourced their IT. Or sometimes it's a combination of both. When it's one individual running IT, some of the work may need to be outsourced.

Almost every time I go in and talk to a company leader about what's wrong, it's the situational dynamic that's at the top of the list. No single person should be expected to fill all the roles required in an IT department.

The company I mentioned in Chapter 1 that called me in for consultation three times in as many years had distinct problems with their IT. None of their technology was working effectively. Everything was slow. They didn't seem to be able to get the results they were looking for. The list of problems and complaints went on for days. I spent hours with upper management explaining, "I think I can help you. Here's what you would have to do," and it involved maximizing the effectiveness of their IT team.

Well, the first time around they didn't take my recommendations. They went ahead and hired more people, fired some, and laid others off. I was called in again the next year to review the new situation, and I gave them the very same advice I had the first time.

The third year I was called in, I cut to the chase about the essentials of putting together a crack team. I offered to study their situation and figure out what it would take for them to put the right team in place. This time they took me up on it. I found out that none of the IT people they'd hired were right for their particular jobs. It was an unfortunate situation that hadn't improved in the three years they'd been looking at it. Regrettably, it could have been avoided or addressed sooner if leadership had taken my advice from the beginning.

So it's easy to see how IT gets a bad rap and winds up being a big source of frustration for CEOs. For the leader of a small company with one IT person, every time he asks for some improvement or upgrade—if he knows enough to ask!—he's told it will cost a bunch of money. Then the project never seems to get done. It just keeps on going and going and going, and it's always over budget.

CEOs and IT people have competing desires. An IT geek is happy to stay up all night building systems. The last thing he wants to do in the morning is help the accounting department with their problems. The bottom line for the CEO is that he doesn't want to have to spend the money. He wants options instead, affordable ones, not the options the IT guy always seems to want.

The Evil in the Machine

Mainframes: The Iron Beast

The evolution of information technology in business tells part of the story of why we think IT is evil. It all begins with mainframe computers, those big iron beasts of the

1960s, '70s, and '80s that filled entire walls and rooms. Mainframes made database technology an integral part of business. Their operation and maintenance required "mad men and women" with specialized training and knowledge who worked as engineers, programmers, and operators. They were the only ones who knew how to control the beast and make it work.

When I first started in the IT world thirty years ago at General Dynamics, all we had were mainframes. There was no way for a typical staff member to move data around. If someone in the organization wanted a printout of a report, the IT people had to do it. We had a backlog of requests years long.

People didn't have their own computers with hard drives. Only a few employees had computer "terminals," and they couldn't do much with them. Everything went through the technology department. Even simple program changes required software development. If you needed a change in a report, you needed IT to make that change for you.

The PC: Personal Computing

The advent of personal computers in the 1980s was a game changer. It allowed the lay user to have control over how he worked. Complete computer novices learned to use desktop PCs that could crunch numbers and get results.

You could write a document using a word-processing program and make your own changes. You could create a spreadsheet, format reports and PowerPoint presentations, and make them pretty. PCs became a tool of work and the home. Computers were no longer the exclusive domain of experts.

PCs operated below the level of mainframes. People were freed from the IT department, even to the point of loading their own programs. It was a new Wild West of computers. And it was beginning to look as if computers weren't so evil after all. All over a company, people stored things on PCs. It was called "distributed computing," but the problem was that there was no continuity whatsoever. There was no central control of data. There was no central repository, which meant there was no central backup. Company data was floating around on floppy disks and USB drives—no security, no protected information.

The solution was for businesses to hook their PCs into network servers, which were network security and backup systems. This new configuration was a whole lot safer. But these new PC networks with their banks of servers in equipment rooms became more like the old-style mainframes again. And people became frustrated again. They had to log into a system to get things done. Companies had a new data beast to deal with. Once again it required the unique skills of specialists trained in the technological dark arts to manage the data.

The Cloud: Pie in the Sky

The introduction of Cloud computing has changed the game once again. Now businesses can store and process data through the Internet with direct access to networks, servers, and applications. The Cloud brings us data storage and access from anywhere. Companies can save on infrastructure costs, and individual PC users can access the Cloud directly. Mobile computing and smartphones are freeing us from the talons of IT.

It's like distributed computing all over again, and with some of the same problems. Nobody knows where everything is. With Cloud computing, one user might load her files to Microsoft OneDrive, another chooses Box, and another prefers Google Docs. It's the new Wild West of computing. Data is strewn all over the place. Individuals may be working on the same thing, but nobody knows what the other guy has done or if they are even on the same version of a document. There's no formal storage for each person.

What about companies that are entirely Cloud based? Cloud computing makes IT management even more complicated than it has ever been. When we used to push the print button at work, there was both an in-house server and a printer. If your document didn't print, you looked at the queue. If you found your job in the queue, you could still force it to go to the printer. Today if you are on Facebook or Quick Books Online and you push the print button and it doesn't print, where do you look? There is no single place to go to figure it out. The print job just got delivered out into the ether. Somewhere somebody probably got that print job, but good luck finding it.

Information technology morphed from the mainframe to the PC, then to the PC network server, and then out to the Cloud, which is like the regular PC again. And the same problems have arisen for the company again: no backups, no security.

No wonder people think IT is evil.

Running From Evil

People are continually trying to get away from the restrictions of IT. They just want to do what they want to do. But as we get away from the restrictions of control, we put ourselves in a position of risk. For the average end user at a company, the risk may not be much, but at the executive level the risks are great and the frustrations even greater.

Take an example of a growing company that starts with ten people and grows to twenty. They do such a good job that they grow to thirty then forty. They also grow in satellite locations. For every ten or twenty people they add, they add another physical location. Every time they add an office, they also need to add routers, firewalls, Internet connectivity, applications, servers, desktops, tablets, Web filters, and security processes.

All of the offices need to be connected, and if the connections don't work, it means downtime for the company. Someone, an architect, has to design it all and make sure it is designed to scale. The fact is, it can take thirty to 120 days or more to get IT installed for a new office. There are many components to a new office: Internet, cabling, equipment, configuring the system, and so on. The CEO isn't planning for all of that. He wants to move in next week. He just wants to open another branch office, and now IT is holding things up.

Information technology has a bad rap because everyone thinks it should be easy. IT should just work. Sure, it's easier today than it's ever been to get things done, but from the perspective of management, it all seems to be getting harder. Why? To answer that question, we have to ask another question: Who drives the development and the shaping of IT?

In today's economy, it's the technology firms that drive the change. Companies such as Microsoft and Google are all about recurring revenue. They just want us to use their tools, and many of them are super cool. Even if they don't charge us for them, they can get a lot of advertising based on how many users are out there.

What's happening today is the awesomeness of the little app. Let's say you just found the coolest app; it works on the Internet or on your tablet or smartphone. It's the best little calendar program on the planet because it's cheap and it works really well. However, it's a standalone. It's not integrated with anything else most of the time. It's a silo. Nobody else in your workplace uses it or even knows about it. These little apps are an IT management challenge. First of all, IT has to support the app if it malfunctions, and that costs the company money. As well, the apps have data associated with them, and that data is not available to other company users who may need to access it. Pretty soon, there is no common place or way to integrate this app's data into the workplace.

Technology is constantly changing. There's always new and newer stuff, and business leaders are overwhelmed by it. They're thinking, how can I run a business when I have to keep running to keep up with technology? That's why it's so frustrating to them.

With today's ever-increasing Internet connectivity, businesses need more advanced security to protect against breaches. I explain to clients that they if they're not careful, somebody could tap into their connectivity for their own purposes. That's the necessary evil part: they don't understand the technology, but they know they're helpless without it. What they don't quite get is that technology is on their side when they *Do IT Right*.

3

How to Mismanage Your IT

Information technology has come a long way since the iron beast mainframes of the 1970s. As we saw in Chapter 2, IT evolved from mainframes to PCs to network servers, and most recently to Cloud computing. All the improvements in technology, speed, and convenience were supposed to make things easier.

In some ways information technology has been democratized. With PCs and laptops, iPads and smartphones, music and video downloads, social networking and more apps than you could ever use, technology is now literally in the hands of the people. At the level of the individual consumer, IT has grown so much easier to use. But at the level of industry, IT just seems to be getting more complex. Ask anyone who's in business, and you'll hear that complaint.

It's Not About the Computer; It's About Connectivity

The fact is, IT is no longer about the computer. It's about connectivity and mobility. Today, mobile technology and applications are in buses and cabs, they're mounted on semitrailers, they're out on the factory floor, and they're on forklifts.

When I ask a company president, "How many people in your organization use computers?" she might say fifteen, thirty, or forty, maybe more. Then if I ask, "How many people in your organization use technology?" she has to give it some thought. I try to get more specific to help her think it through. "Okay, do any of your people use a smartphone for email?" That usually brings a reply, something like, "Well, yeah, all of them do out on the trucks."

So I ask further, "Do they have iPads, too?"

She might say, "Sure, they have iPads. We're mounting them on the dash." Or maybe she'll say, "That's just what I want to talk to you about."

What it boils down to is this: In today's market, IT infrastructure and management needs to extend beyond the office walls. As we've seen so far, IT management has never been easy for business people. Now with super connectivity and mobility, it's only getting harder.

When I do an information technology review for a company, leadership sometimes tries to make a point that those forty staff members using iPads or iPhones aren't relevant to planning processes. So I ask, "What happens if their devices don't work?"

That's a problem they've been avoiding. But how can something so critical to daily operations be excluded from technology management? Wishful thinking. Penny wise and pound foolish. They think it will cost more if they have to manage those devices, too. The fact of the matter is that we're already in an era of mobility. And we're fast approaching an era in time when almost all end users won't be sitting at desks with computers in front of them. Handheld devices may be their only tools for communicating and getting projects done.

The naked, unvarnished truth of today is "Everything is a computer." Part of my job is getting business leaders to realize that and act accordingly. Information technology is ubiquitous; it's everywhere and part of everything. And without appropriate management, IT will fail.

In times past there was no digital technology on a forklift. Factory floors were mechanized, but they didn't have digital robotics. Today there is connectivity in ceilings everywhere, connectivity on forklifts and conveyor belts. There's connectivity at people's fingertips. How do business leaders manage all of that technical complexity? The answer usually is, they don't. This is the big dilemma.

In the not-so-distant past when I first started consulting with businesses, it was primarily about the number of desktop computers in the accounting department, in the finance department, in distribution—and all were on-site locations. Now when a company calls me in, they may have twenty or thirty desktop computers and some laptops, but they've got seventy vans out on the freeway connected and transmitting data. They have a fixed number of people in the office, but they have twice as many on the road or working from home.

How Things Go Wrong

I was called in by a heating, ventilation, and air conditioning (HVAC) company. I set the stage for my discussion with the owner, general manager, and operations manager by asking a few questions: "You called me in to talk about your information technology challenges. What is it that seems to be bothering you? Why am I here today?"

Their response was, "We're completely dependent on technology, and currently we're having trouble communicating by email with our service technicians. Also our billing processes aren't efficient; there seems to be some downtime with our systems. Overall we don't really have a good way to know whether we're getting the kind of service from our information technology providers that we think we should."

So I asked them the question I usually ask: "About how many people, just about—let's just sit here and think about it—are dependent upon technology in your organization?" The first answer they gave me was twenty-five people in the office in operations, customer service, and finance.

So I asked, "How many technicians are out in the field fixing and installing your products?" They gave me a figure of about fifty or more technicians in vehicles with iPhones and iPads, receiving and sending emails. The technicians were dispatched to jobs via application programs, but lately those apps hadn't been working. They'd been having to use the phone, which wastes time and money and was frustrating for everyone. The system had been down for the last week.

The next thing I asked was, "Okay, who's in charge of all that? Who in the company is in charge of field communications, the information technology that's involved in dispatching your technicians?" Everyone just stared at me. Then they kind of looked over at the operations coordinator. I wanted to ask directly, "Are you qualified to be in charge of IT?" but I was more diplomatic. I asked, "What do you do when something doesn't work?" She replied, "I call the IT guys." Their IT was outsourced to a small mom-and-pop shop in the area that provided all of their technological services.

I needed the full picture, so I asked, "As the company has grown and you've implemented these mobile technologies for your technicians out on the road, who has been in charge of planning?" Again came the blank stares. So I asked, "Do you have any kind of a road map for how you're going to get from where you are today to where you want to be in the future?"

I let them mull that over as we talked further. They told me they thought they'd be doubling in size over the next three to five years. They'd already grown, which was fantastic, but they knew they were having issues. So I asked, "How do you intend to double your volume when there's nobody planning the architecture or the services or any of the project implementation?" Their answer was, "That's why you're here, Marty."

They'd gotten as far as they had, "in spite of ourselves," as they bluntly put it. I asked a series of questions to get them thinking:

- How are you planning these new projects?
- How are you planning the rollouts?
- How are you planning your process for determining how long you can go when something doesn't work?
- How much money will you be investing?
- What kind of a return do you expect?

In short, it was time to get down to business.

I explained to these folks that they were never going to get where they wanted to go without treating IT as an integral part of their business plan. I laid out a few fundamentals:

- Planning
- Metrics
- Service levels
- Tracking
- Estimating
- Forecasting

Even if they planned to continue outsourcing their IT, they would still need to put a process of IT management in place.

A Primer on IT Mismanagement

Mismanagement of IT starts when a company fails to treat information technology as part of the usual management process. Companies generally fail to evaluate IT in the manner they evaluate other departments in an organization.

For every other department there is usually an estimate of investment on a yearly basis. There's also some sort of accountability built into the department, accounting for time and project and resource management. There are service requirements and expectations that the job is getting done.

There are all kinds of management structures. Accounting departments are expected to pay vendors on time. If that doesn't happen, it will show in a report as "accounts payable aging." When vendors haven't been paid for thirty, sixty, ninety, 120 days or more, management will know that something is amiss.

Companies have the same requirements for accounts receivable. There's a process in place for collecting money owed for goods and services. It's done on a monthly or more frequent basis. Organizations typically want to have their books closed and the month ended inside of a week following a given month.

Accountability, service levels, and processes are understood as traditional business functions. Unfortunately, companies don't view IT in the same way. Particularly when IT is outsourced, management doesn't pay it enough attention. They don't have a good sense of expectations for their IT. As described in Chapter 2, they view it as a necessary evil they'd prefer to have as little to do with as possible. They haven't considered metrics for measuring IT efficiency or effectiveness.

Consider the shipping department of a distribution company. Orders flow out either on paper or digitally via computer applications. Orders go to the department that picks, packs, and ships. Managers of that department make sure that their products get on a truck for delivery to the customer in the time it takes to meet their goals. When you order a product online with Amazon, you've chosen your shipping method and you know your approximate delivery date. You can even track your item online. Managers in charge of order fulfillment know the measure of their success. Did they get that item to you in the promised time, and undamaged? They'll know when something goes wrong. If the item isn't in stock, they'll let you know from the get-go.

It's a pretty basic process, however complicated it may be to actually make it happen. It involves multiple people along the fulfillment chain and a whole lot of software to receive and route the order to your door. Distribution knows exactly what they're doing, and management knows how to measure their success.

However, when it comes to IT, if the boss asks, "What can I expect from you when it comes to service delivery, planning, and best practices?" they are met with a blank stare.

In the case of the HVAC company mentioned earlier, management assures the customer of the purchase, delivery, and installation of their new heating or air conditioning system. They've evaluated the job, made their bid, and contracted with the customer on certain agreed terms. All parties know when installation will take place. Management knows when the product and equipment will be available and on the truck. They know the timeframe, and they know their personnel and what it will take to get the job done. They know which service technicians will be available, how many they'll need, and which combination of people will work best. They probably know down to the hour how long the job will take. They have established processes for bidding, scheduling, and executing the job. They wouldn't want to do it any other way. They need to be able to assure the customer that the new system will be up and running on a certain date. Management can tell you how many times a month they do similar jobs and get them done on time.

Both in the distribution example of Amazon and the service example of HVAC, management has clear metrics in place. They have quantifiable measures to track and assess the status of the particular business processes. In each case, there are dozens of individual metrics needed to measure and evaluate process, efficiency, and cost. Both company management and staff know they will be held accountable. There are no surprises.

However, when it comes to information technology, management is at a loss. It's not that they need to know all the specifics of how to build a server or how to put up a Cloud application. But they do need to plan for those needs, how long they will take, and what they will cost.

In the long term, management needs to develop an IT plan that keeps pace with growth. They need to know what kind of investment they'll need to make in IT two, three, and five years out. They don't want to find out halfway through the growth process that they have to slow down in order to wait for their technology to catch up. They need to allocate the funding for that growth in advance.

Management needs to know how IT will address problems as they arise. They need to plan for exigencies. If something isn't working, how long on average will it take to get it working again? How does the company function during downtime? In the case of complete system failure, what has to be done and how long will it take to fix it? They need to account for service levels and for compliance with industry rules. Compliance is a metric in and of itself. For instance, a company that takes payment with credit cards must be PCI compliant. Health-care organizations must adhere to HIPAA compliance. All require metrics. How many computers are patched on a daily basis with security patches? Is the firewall up to date? Is the Web filter up to date? Management needs the kind of reporting that tells them where they stand.

Company managers need appropriate reporting and benchmarking of IT for smooth functioning. It's a matter of operational effectiveness. For every minute a staff member waits for in-house or outsourced IT to come deal with a situation, that staff member isn't working. Low productivity adds costs to doing business.

Dangers of Mismanagement

When I consult with clients, we do a technology review of their entire IT infrastructure. Time and time again, I find that management has a hard time grasping the fact that tablets and smartphones should be included in the IT planning process. What happens if employees' devices don't work? What happens if they can't communicate? It becomes a company problem. The upshot is that anything critical to a company's daily operations should not be excluded from technology management.

I was called in to consult with a company of some four hundred end users. They had a pretty good IT team in place of three or four people, but their IT system wasn't reliable. The operations manager told me that every day there was another problem. We had a long discussion in which I laid out the primary IT functions, the actual jobs that it takes to do the backroom management of IT infrastructure. These are the essential behind-the-scenes tasks of keeping the engine running. I also spoke with the IT team, and as things stood, nobody really had a handle on those vital backroom functions. On a day-to-day basis, the tasks were going unmonitored. It was another case of mismanagement. The IT team had a pretty good handle on end users and business applications, but the critical guts of their IT infrastructure were being neglected.

By the way, a "line of business application" or "enterprise application" is the primary program that runs an organization. In a mortgage company you would have a program that helps make loans. In a CPA firm you'd have a program that helps track the billing for clients, as well as financial statements and tax returns. Law offices have legal systems that help create pleadings and other court-related needs. Distribution companies and manufacturers have business applications that help them track tools and processes, materials and inventories. Business applications are very necessary to the functioning of the company. If you're in business, you depend on those applications to run smoothly. When the IT team isn't covering all the bases, and the management team doesn't know which bases to cover, the company leadership is just asking for trouble.

It can take a while for companies to notice how bad things have gotten. Start-ups tend to think they can get almost everything for free on the Internet. Things don't seem too complicated in the beginning. But when it comes to the task of manufacturing your product, or getting your legal systems up and running, or getting a medical-practice management system up and running and keeping it running, things become more complicated. And when it comes to security and viruses, mismanagement becomes a business hazard. IT mismanagement occurs in many of these areas. Companies may try to put off the installation of expensive firewalls to save money, but they reach a point when it's a whole lot cheaper to *Do IT Right*. When companies grow in size, the effects of mismanagement become more apparent.

Let's say that the firm you started with three people has grown to thirty people. At first, document management was as simple as Google Docs. But over time, documents are stored in so many locations that staff begin expressing confusion. You start to need a more robust document-management system. Your workplace is changing, and so are your IT needs. There's also a greater need for document security, and security over all.

Prospective clients are always telling me how frustrated they are. One of their main complaints is they don't know what options they have. They feel over a barrel with IT. They feel damned if they do try to improve IT, because they don't really know a better way. They're not even sure if their IT person or IT team knows. And they feel damned if they don't try to improve IT, because the less they do about it, the worse things seem to get. They want to know if they're spending the right amount of money. Are they getting a reasonable return on investment? What would happen in the case of a disaster—would they be able to recover their information? What would happen if the IT people quit? Is everything secure? Are they safe from the threats of today's Internet world? These business leaders are starting to lose sleep with worry.

For those companies that need to protect proprietary and confidential information for competitive advantage or for customer privacy or for compliance with the law, IT security is essential. Mismanaging their information technology is sheer neglect. They need to have the right people with the right expertise in place in-house, or they need to outsource to reputable vendors.

A security breach is certainly a dramatic consequence of IT mismanagement. Other consequences may be less damaging in the short term, but harmful over time.

Sometimes it's raw fear that prompts managers or CEOs to call for a consultation. Often it's because something has gone wrong and can't be put off any longer. They know they need help. They're afraid things will snowball into fatality. "Can you take a look and see?" they ask me. So we go and have a look and find out that they don't have any backup. Their system has been infected with the new CryptoLocker virus, a ransomware Trojan that sneaks in through infected email attachments. It locks up files in a way that users can't access their own files without paying a ransom. One way to get rid of the malware is to restore files over the top with backup files. But in this case they had no backups.

That's what business leaders worry about: Are they secure, and do they have a way back in when something goes wrong? In the short term, they need a fix. What I try to explain is that in the long term, they have an IT management problem. Mismanagement has brought them to this crossroads, and it's time to make some critical choices.

A Rudderless Ship

For a company like Amazon, IT isn't a "necessary evil." It isn't merely necessary; it's integral and vital to their operations. IT is part and parcel of Amazon's business model. Mismanagement of IT is as foreign to Amazon as receiving checks and cash in the mail as payment for merchandise.

My work has shown me that far too many business leaders believe all is well with their technology as long as nobody is complaining. That's a very low bar. When a problem arises and I'm called in for a consultation, I explain, "If you think the way you're handling IT now will help you reach your goals, you're just setting yourself up for more disappointment." Many clients still just want a simple fix for a recurring problem. They're afraid to spend money upfront for increased efficiency.

As I'll show in Chapter 4, effective management of IT can actually lower a company's IT costs. Those CEOs who are reluctant to make the systemic changes in management are basically just kicking the can down the road. All too often I'll be meeting with them again a year later going over the same problems or new and different problems stemming from the same mismanagement.

The problem with IT mismanagement is that it runs against not only a company's goals, but its vision. CEOs, business owners, and presidents are their company's leaders. They set the agenda, the objectives, the policies, the targets, and the company's mission. They are truly the captains of their ship. They've hired a crew that depends on them for a paycheck and career advancement. When they fail at the level of IT management, they are in fact failing the company. When they disappoint the expectations of the crew, when the winds are not in their sails or the ship goes aground, morale is low. Productivity is low. The company's problem becomes the crew's problem, but it's really the CEO's problem. Mismanagement at any level of a company puts the company ship at risk.

Company leadership bears the blame because that's where the buck stops. When a business leader delegates responsibility for information technology to an IT person or team, or to an outsourced vendor, he can't wash his hands of it. He is still responsible to see that the job gets done, that the ship doesn't take on water.

Here's how mismanagement can steer a ship into the shoals. I was consulted by a friend who is the CEO of a small company. He told me he was having a very difficult time contracting new clients and selling new business. A few years back his company had been doing much better, but since then growth had slowed. In fact, his business had begun to shrink. I told him, "Let's try an experiment. Let me send you this personality test." It's the one I mentioned in Chapter 2, the same personality test I use for hiring at my own company.

He took the test, and when I looked at the results I was amazed. The test showed that he had a strong builder personality and a strong innovator personality. Yet, it also showed that he had no merchant personality whatsoever. That was the root of his problem. He was failing at closing new business, and he was his company's salesperson! I told him, "Look, here's what you've got to do. You have to hire a kick-butt salesperson and a team to back him up. Share your knowledge of how you build things, how you innovate, share your vision and goals, and make sure the sales team can run with it.

What drives the mismanagement of IT is the same kind of neglect and inattention to detail that drives business mismanagement in general. It's the failure to apply basic business principles and processes. Some very smart people fail to study the charts, plot their course, and steer the company ship. They hire their IT crew and leave it up to them, but they fail on the management side.

Almost every time I talk to a company leader about what

is wrong with his or her company's IT, it turns out that it's the situation that's wrong. More often than not, they've staffed the department incorrectly. It sets them up for problems right from the start.

That's why I'm always telling my clients, "IT isn't about computers; it's about business management."

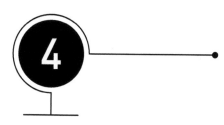

Get the Most From Your IT

We've seen how CEOs and business leaders unintentionally ignore IT management. Information technology can be intimidating to people with little or no technical background. The upshot is that business leaders fail to approach IT from a management perspective. They tend to fall short of effectively managing their IT person, department, and resources.

The question is: What can a CEO do to get the most from IT?

My theory of getting great results from information technology is to manage IT as you would any other department in your organization. Management is where the rubber hits the road in business. Excellent management helps business people achieve effective results. If you don't do a good job of managing your business as a whole, there's little chance of getting effective results from your technology. IT enters into every aspect of a company. Every department from finance to marketing depends on software applications, connectivity, and system safety. Effective management therefore requires particular attention to IT management.

When it comes to technology, the management principles I have adopted are very much, if not exactly, the same as the universal principles of good management. Adopting effective management is the key to getting awesome results from your IT and your business in general.

Solid Management Principles

Smart business leaders school themselves in solid management principles.

Peter Drucker, known as the "founder of modern management," stressed the importance of management as leadership. For Drucker, effective management begins with hiring the best people, understanding the customer, and refining competitive advantages. His seminal book, *The Practice of Management*, set the stage for a new way of thinking about business management.

Drucker believed that the role of management is to make the team function. Managers have to accept responsibility and not sidestep. He insisted that "a manager is responsible for the application and performance of knowledge." Experience showed him that "what is measured improves." Leadership, he insisted, is "defined by results."

Drucker was regularly consulted by America's corporate leaders, including Jack Welch of General Electric (GE), who had his own theories of management. Welch's motivational goal was to make every division of GE top in its class. Under his leadership, the market value of GE increased from $12 billion to $505 billion. Welch understood that managers should never ignore the facts on the ground. When they do, they fail. They need to constantly weigh their business environment, their market, and new technology.

Verne Harnish, author of *Mastering the Rockefeller Habits*, stresses "data" as one of his three pillars of management. In his thinking, daily and weekly feedback in the form of concrete numbers and stats helps a company navigate the market. Otherwise companies are buffeted by crosswinds. Harnish advocates accountability and dashboards because the only way to properly manage is to measure. His emphasis on metrics is similar to Drucker's.

Optimize IT

Business leaders understand, sometimes reluctantly, that information technology is necessary for conducting business in the digital age. Although many still see it as a "necessary evil," as described in Chapter 2, IT isn't only necessary—it's critical.

What business leaders sometimes fail to see is that IT is a business asset. And when information technology is mismanaged, a company's IT falls short. It fails to deliver as an asset. When you do things better than your competition, when you outperform your competition in any way, shape, or form, you increase your market share, and frequently lower your costs. Strategic investment can yield efficiencies that lower the costs of manufacturing and the delivery of goods and services.

IT shouldn't be put on the back burner. It can't simply be left to staff or outsourced without oversight. It's essential to move information technology to the front burner. It's what your competition is doing. If you're not paying attention to technology management, you risk falling behind the curve in your industry. You won't be optimizing your results. Instead, your competition will be able to move more quickly to seize the advantage. They will compete more swiftly to maximize their own market share.

For example, a mechanical contractor who has a dynamic process of IT management in place can run his service vans and technicians with increased efficiency. His company has built-in safeguards that keep his people on the road repairing and installing machinery. Business volume is higher, customers are happy, technicians are happy, the support team is happy, and the owner is happy.

A distribution company with an effective warehouse-management system has the competitive advantage. Increased efficiency lowers both labor costs and shipping costs while increasing customer satisfaction.

When Amazon throws its considerable weight behind drone-delivery technology, they aren't just throwing around money to look good. They are seeking to maximize their IT advantage because they want to lower delivery costs, decrease delivery time, and increase customer satisfaction. They want to be on the leading edge of their industry, which is selling and delivering on the sale. They pride themselves on it. IT is simply good business.

Align IT With Your Business Plan

A company that fumbles with mismanaged IT processes will be left in the dustbin of history. When managed correctly, information technology acts as a springboard to launch a business forward. A company gains strategic advantage when it embraces IT.

A company's IT plan needs to work in concert with its overarching business plan. A company that neglects to align its IT with its business strategy will not meet its goals. Remember, IT is not about the computer; it's really about business processes. A company that wants to grow needs an effective business plan aligned with its IT. Technology that aligns with business strategy always delivers better results.

Smart companies that plan for growth always align their funding with IT and strategy. A company that plans to grow 10, 20, or 50 percent, whatever their goal, has to keep pace with information technology, otherwise they'll be playing catch-up. When information technology falls behind, the IT department goes crazy. A company that grows fast and fails to align its funding with IT will hit a roadblock. An IT department that isn't prepared will be in reactive mode. It frustrates CEOs and business leaders when their IT falls behind. But it's a failure of management when IT isn't aligned with goals in the planning stage.

For a company that expects to grow by two hundred people next year, it's not as simple as plugging in two hundred more computers. Good management will communicate expectations and include IT in the planning process. A company's website, advertising, and marketing will all be involved in that growth. All departments need to be closely aligned with IT. When companies fail to plan in this way, they wind up chasing their own tail. Their IT department will be right behind them doing the same thing. Unfortunately, too many smart managers have blinders on when it comes to IT. They need to understand that information technology is not about fixing broken stuff; it's about growing a business.

An effective business plan takes IT into account when setting quarterly goals for the company. Each short-term goal builds upon the next to reach the company's long-term goals. A goal may be as basic and effective as IT documentation. A well-conceived strategic plan includes a timeframe for quarterly, yearly, and multiple-year goals. IT goals are prioritized first by what *must* get done and then by what is *desired*. Need goes before want. IT goals should be reached by specific dates. The cost is calculated upfront.

By the way, it's convenient to show metrics, data, and processes visually with dashboards. Dashboards are great management tools. They chart and graph key performance indicators (KPIs) that can show at a glance all the measurable trends, as well as the necessary IT maintenance that will be needed over time.

Any single objective for IT may be broken down into component parts to reach that objective. For example, let's say you have a server that is ten years old. There's a risk that it will break down. We don't know if it will, but it might. If it does break, the risk is downtime. Downtime can delay delivery of a product or service. On a dashboard, equipment replacement would show visually in bright red. It can't be missed. It must be dealt with in a timely fashion. The old server is scheduled for replacement, and the cost has been estimated. In the IT business plan, details of the process have been outlined. IT technicians will handle the buying of equipment and installation, as well as the programming and transfer of data. On the management side, the maintenance has been planned, cost-estimated, and scheduled. On the technology side, IT has participated in the planning, earmarked the maintenance, and will see to the work.

In this way, management synchronizes business growth with IT. When management has a definite plan and strategy, they can build in their metrics, those quantifiable measures to track and assess their business processes.

Take, for example, a company that has forecast growth for the next year to include one hundred new end users. The line item in the IT business plan would indicate an increase in infrastructure capacity by a certain amount and a certain date. Details are delineated leading up to that date. It may take the IT department four quarters to get there. Each of those quarters will have its own objectives designed to reach the goal of supporting those one hundred new end users.

With a well-conceived strategic plan, a manager can proceed according to defined milestones and dates. Tasks can be assigned. The manager can determine who needs which resources and when. The IT team keeps to the timetable of the dashboard. Management can huddle daily, weekly, and monthly with the IT team to confirm that tasks are still doable in accordance with the established timetable. They may also decide whether adjustments need to be made. It's not uncommon to underestimate the number of steps involved to complete a particular task. When the details of a task come to light in real time, some tweaking and modification of the timetable may be necessary. Conversely, an objective may seem more complicated on paper, but turn out to be far more simple to accomplish. The implementation of strategic plans therefore involves some adaptability in real time. The important thing is that the plan is there. The company's goals and course of growth have been plotted and aligned with IT. Performance indicators have been established. Everyone knows what is expected of them.

For example, at my own company, our twelve-person leadership team came together in January to finish our strategic plan. We were looking at the tasks. One of the tasks caught my eye, and I asked, "Can we get this done in ninety days?" The project manager started going through the various components of the task, which turned out to be far more than we'd originally considered. The projection of ninety days had been way off the mark. We concluded that it would be next to impossible to complete even in a whole year. We ended up redoing the timetable and spreading out the milestones for completion over a more realistic period of time.

A comprehensive strategic business plan will break down quarterly goals into weekly objectives. Yearly goals, and goals for five years and even ten years out, will also be broken down into smaller increments. Those steps are mapped out toward the completion of the goal. The strategic plan is a living document that management uses to keep pace and make changes according to realities on the ground. For short-term tasks or more complicated tasks, the team may huddle frequently to evaluate its progression.

Security: The Canary in the IT Coal Mine

Every CEO should arrange to have an IT security audit

done by a consulting firm. Security is one of the few areas that immediately reveals at a very basic level how well a company's IT is being managed. Typically, CEOs and business people like to believe that their IT is just fine. If there haven't been problems lately, then things must be all right, right? Wrong. Security is at the heart of a company's IT. If an audit shows deficiencies at the fundamental level of security, the CEO will know that IT has a management problem.

Simple security-maintenance procedures generally lock most of the virtual doors to an organization—not all of them, but most. More advanced IT security procedures protect against a greater number of attacks, hacks, and phishing that can infect an organization and compromise data. But when I'm called in for a consultation, what I usually find is the organization has done very few of the basics. Even when there's an information technology department in place, security is below par. From a technology standpoint, security is simple. It's not the most complicated part of IT. On the level of email phishing, it's more complicated, but the basics are pretty straightforward.

The very basics of security start outside an organization at their firewall. A firewall is a system that prevents unauthorized access to a company's private network. It includes both hardware and software. The number-one principle of a firewall is that it must be up to date. What I find most often, however, is that installed firewalls aren't updated. They are functioning at a level of risk.

The next element of security is a Web filter. It keeps bad things from coming in and sometimes from going out. The filter is programmed with rules that say what should happen if something comes in that shouldn't be there. It also protects against people misusing the system from within, going places on the Web where they shouldn't and compromising the organization. At the level of compliance and law, Web filters protect business owners from potential lawsuits involving employee indiscretion.

Security is also vital at the level of workstations and devices that connect to the company's network and the Internet. At this end-user level, security needs to be updated daily, weekly, and monthly. Here's where antivirus software, Microsoft patches, and Apple patches need to be in place.

Surprisingly, even in companies that have IT departments in place, security is lacking. Every time I see it, I'm taken aback. This is why I encourage every CEO to invest minimally in a security assessment by a reputable IT consultant. Security assessments reveal so much about both the state of a company's defenses and its IT management.

A deficiency in security is the canary in the IT coal mine.

Spotting Problems

A secure IT environment is one in which employees are using IT resources and tools in a way that benefits the company. When it comes to staff using services such as Spotify or Pandora at work, management has an overriding interest—not so much in an employee's musical tastes, but in the company's Internet resources.

The number-one complaint I hear from clients is that their Internet is slow. When thirty or a hundred company's end users are listening to Spotify, watching the news, using Pandora, or watching YouTube videos, every one of them is using the company's bandwidth. It doesn't take very many to slow the whole system down. It's a matter of resource allocation. A business's wireless system is providing streaming music. Of course, listening to music at work, when it doesn't interfere with getting work done, is good for morale. But I have walked into organizations where two or three users are streaming videos, which use a lot of bandwidth, and it stops fifty other users from working at all.

Recently an organization called me in to help them resolve a slow Internet connection. The first thing we did was turn off four iPhones that were constantly accessing the company's wireless system. The managers had no idea that was even a consideration. It was such a simple fix.

It falls to management to control the environment and get results. When managers or end users have to call for IT help, it takes them away from doing their jobs. Effective IT management demands a proactive, not a reactive, mindset. If you're planning for the proper maintenance processes and implementing best practices at all levels of your organization, you're ahead of the game. Your productivity goes way up.

A simple solution is for staff to use their own wireless connections, such as Verizon. They still get their music, but now they're paying for it themselves and not impacting day-to-day business operations.

Quiet Management

A well-managed IT environment is quiet. It isn't disruptive. There is none of what we call in the trade "technology noise." Technology noise is all the hustle and bustle of running around trying to get hardware and software and doing installations to tackle problems. IT staff winds up having to kick users out of the way, crowding their workstations because the fix has to get done today. The boss says so. So they are on the phone calling Internet suppliers and vendors for technical support. They're ordering computers and trying to get them in. It's all super chaotic.

But when IT is managed correctly, information technology is quiet. When maintenance and upgrades and growth are planned in advance, the IT environment is streamlined. It's more like a bullet train than a city bus making stops at every corner.

Many of the organizations I've worked with have turned their IT problems around. They've taken their IT to new levels of efficiency, and they are reaping the rewards of productivity. The distribution company that plans for and implements a new warehouse-management system competes at a high level and beats the competition at delivery times.

It's the Amazon model that I mentioned earlier. The reason Amazon is so successful at business is they're so advanced technologically. You don't have to invest to the degree that Amazon invests in IT, but you have to use IT to scale your business.

Think Like a CIO

Whether or not a company has a chief information officer depends on its size. Only larger companies invest in the expense of a full-time CIO to oversee information technology management and resources. It's an issue of affordability. What every company needs, however, is someone who *thinks* like a CIO.

CIOs can see the big picture. They are deeply involved in IT planning. They plan short- and long-term goals and strategize for the future. They budget and plan in advance for the most effective IT framework at every stage of a company's growth. CIOs plan ahead for the purchase of new IT equipment and system upgrades. They map out IT strategy and are responsible for the recruitment of IT staff.

The perspective of CIOs is above the trees. They can see the proverbial tree and the forest. In other words, while they see the big picture, they don't miss the details. They put the best IT people in place to see to the day-to-day functioning and maintenance of hardware, software, security, and information systems. They make sure the company's IT business plan is funded, metrics are in place, and tasks are executed on a definitive timetable.

One of my team members recently boarded a plane to go meet with a software developer for sawmills. Why on earth would one of my consultants go to a sawmill? The client is a lumber yard, and the CFO is thinking about implementing new software to increase productivity and distribution, and also to limit waste. Three members of the company's management team will meet with my technical specialist who is acting as their CIO. He'll be on-site at the sawmill to see how the software could potentially work.

A company's CIO, or an outsourced fractional CIO, engages in an ongoing business process to evaluate, identify, and develop the company's IT infrastructure and network. He positions IT to meet the company's objectives for expansion and takes responsibility for IT projects necessary for reaching the company's short-term and long-term objectives.

A Trusted Advisor

When CEOs and business leaders ask me how to get the most from their IT, I often recommend that they consult an IT advisor. Many entrepreneurs enlist advisors or mentors as part of their professional support network. A trusted technology advisor can be a business colleague, perhaps a CIO or chief technology officer (CTO), or an established entrepreneur who has learned the ropes of managing IT for his or her own company. The advisor can be a business coach or a consultant.

What IT advisors bring to the table is expertise or experience that is applicable to different business situations. They can help think through the possibilities and variables involved in IT decision-making and management. They've been there before and have stories to tell, good and bad, and always instructive. A trusted advisor is an invaluable resource.

Business people need to know their options when it comes to IT. In the next chapter, we'll be looking more deeply at those options.

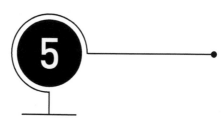

From Problem to Strategic Asset

At the level of the boots on the ground, there are basically three ways for a company to manage and implement its information technology:

- In-house
- Outsource
- Hybrid

In-house IT is done by an individual or team of employees on the company payroll. Outsourcing is a different approach involving no internal IT staff. The work is contracted to outside consultants. The hybrid option is a combination of both with some IT functions done by staff working in-house and others outsourced to consultants. All three have distinct benefits and drawbacks, pros and cons.

A practical and well-reasoned approach to IT can make all the difference in a company transforming its information technology from a problem to a strategic business asset. So let's take a look at the three models of IT implementation and management.

In-House

The Pros

With in-house IT, a company has all of their staff support right on-site. All of the necessary support for infrastructure, line of business applications, systems, and networks is nearby. The IT team or individual is in the next office providing everything it takes to deliver technology to the firm's end users. They are available at a moment's notice.

The IT team that works directly for their employer gains an institutional knowledge, which makes them even more valuable to the organization. They can work on all sorts of internal projects. The in-house IT team also gains daily familiarity with a company's systems, requirements, and even peculiarities.

The in-house team knows the staff. They are coworkers

and share a sense of loyalty and commitment to the company. They know they will sink or swim with the company. They are also on hand to deal with the small stuff—printer jams, loose connections, bad plugs.

An internal team has more flexibility when it comes to services and business processes, so they can respond to change more quickly. They respond faster to fluctuations in demand. They can be there at a moment's notice. With an in-house team, a company's core IT capability is available at the ready to set strategy and maximize competitive advantage.

The Cons

At the top of the list of drawbacks of in-house IT is cost. The expense of salary and benefits, office and equipment, for several full-time employees can be twice the cost of outsourcing. By necessity, as the company grows, the in-house team grows, too. That one full-time salary grows to two, then three, and so on as responsibilities become more specialized and complex.

In the case of companies that have a single individual on staff, there are too many responsibilities and technical challenges for one person to handle. There tends to be a backlog of requests for the help desk, as well as for the implementation of projects and other areas of technology.

A small team can feel bombarded by end users and the expanding scope of work.

There's also a tendency for small in-house teams to think short-term. Problems arise and so they deal with what's most immediate. They're so busy chasing problems that their long-term focus falls short. Planning and strategizing doesn't get done. It's all about getting through the day. The result is that the company's long-term IT strategy and goals suffer.

As mentioned in previous chapters, in-house IT departments are inclined to build small empires. A single IT person will lobby for more hires, more experts on the team. He's tired of the help desk and wants to work on software. He's bored. What he really wants to do is manage the network. He's looking for growth potential. Employers wind up having to deal with the management of a group of individuals they don't really understand.

From the start, CEOs of small companies lack the expertise necessary to hire talented IT managers or staff. They are not aware that an IT person working solo needs to engage in planning and strategizing with management. IT isn't just about technical skills. There's so much more involved than software, hardware, and systems. Someone who's good at the help desk and troubleshooting end-user problems may be in the dark when it comes to diagnosing network security issues or upgrading the server. All of which is why in-house IT frequently falls short. It goes back to the failures of management discussed in Chapter 3.

Outsource

The Pros

As we've seen throughout this book, a company's core competency is usually in its own industry, not information technology. When IT is outsourced, all of the day-to-day tasks, including installation of software and hardware, information systems, security and firewalls, network administration, maintenance, upgrades, and technology management, are taken care of by professional IT consultants. Company management does not have to create their own best practices. Instead, best practices are defined beforehand by professionals who do it all the time. Many outsourcers and professional IT service providers have spent millions of dollars developing best practices and customizing management tools.

Another benefit of outsourcing is that results are usually consistent. This is because an outsourcer is already in the business of measuring their own activity. It's in their business interest to try to make IT consistently better for their clients.

An established IT outsourcer draws upon its own team of experts. A fractional team of experts delivers technology in a broad range of disciplines. "Fractional" in this sense refers to distinctive IT skills and jobs. IT experts may be skilled in software engineering, computer programming, systems, networks, operations, or help-desk support, among many other areas of specialization. Of course, some IT professionals have multiple skills and wear more than one hat, but their heads are only so big. No single individual is an expert in everything IT. For a smaller organization there's a definite benefit to not having to hire an entire in-house staff of experts, or to depend on one IT person's brain and capability for every IT situation; this puts the IT person on staff in an impossible situation.

An IT outsourcer dispatches experts on a fractional, as-needed basis. It's usually considerably less expensive for a company than hiring a whole team of internal IT staff members. This is a major plus for a business's bottom line.

For companies that need to manage their overarching technology, including projects and infrastructure, websites and software development projects, outsourcing offers tangible and readily accessible solutions. Outsourcers give companies the full spectrum of IT management. They understand that it takes a village to execute the technology management process. It takes more than a single individual or two.

IT consultants are hardware and software experts, delivery experts, and are highly experienced in tracking metrics. One reason they're so good at what they do is that they have to prove their worth to their clients daily, weekly, monthly, and yearly. If they don't excel at what they are contracted to do, their client will find another contractor to do it better. Letting a consultant go and finding a new one is a whole lot easier than having to reshuffle or lay off staff.

Outsourcers have the ability to handle custom situations. Their pool of experts is large enough and versatile enough to scale support options to meet individual client needs. In an organization where there's a small IT department on staff, if one end user is getting help from the help desk, it means another end user who needs help has to wait. That's downtime. It lowers productivity. Outsourcing offers a solution to that.

IT consultants can scale their resources to the immediate and long-term needs of their clients. They operate from a dynamic of efficiency. A small manufacturer or distribution company can't afford to hire three help-desk people today when end user demand is high, then let two of them go tomorrow when there are fewer problems. An outsourcer can balance that demand and supply, dispatching their own experts on an as-needed basis.

Another advantage is that the client never has to worry about their outsourcer calling in sick. IT consultants have a sizable team to draw upon to deliver experts on-site and remotely in a moment's notice to clients. The client doesn't have to worry about hiring and interviewing applicants, paying a benefits package, or offering sick time or vacation time.

It's important to note, however, that even when IT is outsourced, the ultimate responsibility for IT and setting a company's strategic direction still remains in-house. The company needs to engage with their outside consultants to develop short- and long-term IT goals and an informed strategic plan. There's no passing the buck when it comes to IT and strategy management.

The Cons

Of course, all is not rosy on the outsourcing side. IT outsourcers are set up to deliver services for the most common client needs and situations. Services and scale, or size, of services are sometimes more customizable in theory than in fact. Not all IT outsourcers are created equal. A company may have special needs that are difficult for an outsourcer to jump on. The task may be too far from their range of services.

It's like an auto-mechanic garage set up to work on domestic cars. Someone drives in with a Ferrari. The garage has excellent technicians who do great work, but not on foreign models. They aren't going to hire one guy to work exclusively on Ferraris. It wouldn't be cost-effective. Even among garages that specialize in foreign cars, only a few work on Ferraris. Similarly, IT consultants may be equipped to customize their services for clients, but not in every case. Scrambling to implement services for a particular client may be too costly for the outsourcer.

In some situations, outsourcing can leave a hole. A company manager can't simply go get his IT guy from the next office and say, "Hey, what do you think about this?" If the company's IT is outsourced, that guy isn't going to be there.

However, a good outsourcer will have a fractional chief information officer that will fill that void. The great IT service providers focus on the practice of providing fractional CIOs and see this practice as a competitive advantage for the client and the IT firm.

Another important drawback to outsourcing IT pertains to specialized business knowledge in a particular industry. A mortgage company might prefer to have an IT specialist on staff who really understands mortgage software. Business software is specific and not general. It isn't email or even a common business software like spreadsheets. It's a line of business application that requires specific expertise. An outside IT consultant may not have that specialist in their pool. On the other hand, a good outsourcer will take the time to learn that mortgage software. He would train more than one member of his team in the institutional knowledge required to service, maintain, and troubleshoot that software, so someone would always be on hand to deal with it.

Hybrid

The Pros

The hybrid approach is a partnership between outsourcing and in-house staff. It combines the strengths of both approaches to IT while eliminating some of the weaknesses, cost, and duplication of effort.

Let's say a distribution company has three hundred end users. They depend on software that helps them deliver products every single day. The company has very specific processes and a line of business application that helps them get the job done. These elements of IT are best managed by internal experts with deep knowledge of the product. A one- or two-person internal IT team can best see to the management of the full line of business support. The results will be high because the in-house staff is focused on the business end.

At the same time, the company will outsource what is called the "commodity" elements of IT. These will be the help desk, network administration, monitoring, patching, security, and other functions. All of the routine maintenance functions can be done effectively and more cheaply by outside consultants. Typically, the results are high.

The outsourcer offers fresh perspective and helps free up time for the in-house team to concentrate more on business goals, objectives, and strategy. In this model, the in-house team focuses more on development and core business, while the consultants manage the servers, security, Cloud, and networks. And when the internal team gets stuck, they have the security of a backup team of people who are already in tune with the company's systems and processes.

When done correctly, the hybrid model can be an extremely cost-effective approach.

The Cons

On the other hand, when not done correctly, the hybrid model can just be more costly. The company is paying high in-house salaries and benefits for its line of business experts and paying consulting fees at the same time.

On the outsourced side, of course, there are no recruiting costs, payroll, or health insurance to pay, but there may be hidden costs. Companies should be clear beforehand whether or not there are additional per-incident fees for services. When companies rely on outsourcers, there's also a tendency to overinvest in technology. A company may overspend beyond its real IT needs.

In the beginning there may be some coordination issues. Best practices have to be implemented, and lines have to be clearly drawn. There needs to be clear delineation between what the outsourcer will do and what the internal team will do. Once the lines are in place, the hybrid model can be very efficient and effective, as long as everybody understands the edges. Once all of the team members from the internal group and the external team are synced up and the feelings of insecurity are extinguished, this can be a great option for IT in organizations with complicated technology.

Which Is Best?

I have seen all three models work for different kinds and sizes of businesses.

Small Firms

Smaller organizations benefit considerably by outsourcing their IT. They usually don't have the funds to field an in-house team. IT consultants operate from a dynamic of efficiency. They can scale their resources to the immediate and long-term needs of their clients. A small company can't afford to hire multiple help-desk people when end-user demand is high, then let them go when there are fewer problems. An outsourcer can balance that demand, dispatching their own experts on an as-needed basis.

Also, as we've seen throughout this book, an IT staff member working solo tends to pick and choose among the ever-broadening range of responsibilities. He's busy doing what he likes and lobbying for projects that might not be the most important to the company.

Smaller organizations also may find it cost prohibitive to implement a hybrid model. A company of fewer than one hundred employees may benefit best by outsourcing their IT for less money.

Midsize Firms

Most any midsize company can benefit by outsourcing everything from day-to-day tasks to information systems, security, and technology management. Results tend to be consistent, and the company can depend on the outsourcer to pay attention to metrics and key IT performance indicators. As management partners, outsourcers can be relied on for best practices and a track record of results. They have the fractional expertise to deliver consistently across the areas of IT specialization.

Large Firms

The larger the company, say one thousand or more users, the more they would benefit from a diverse in-house staff of IT specialists. An in-house team can be counted on for strategic development and core business, while also seeing to the commodities, such as servers, Cloud, security, the help desk, and networks.

The greater overall expense of staffing in-house IT can be absorbed more readily by a large company than by a small or midsize firm. Larger companies can reap the benefits of in-house IT, including on-site staff support for infrastructure and line of business applications. Institutional knowledge and proprietary information remain inside the company, which enhances security. The flexibility of an internal team and its ability to meet fluctuations in demand adds to the firm's competitive advantage. Strategizing and planning remain completely in-house, as does accountability. However, even large organizations can take advantage of outsourcing routine tasks, which will most likely save payroll dollars.

Three Case Studies

Doing the Math

On one occasion I was called in by the chief financial officer of a small manufacturing company. His complaint concerned the internal operations of his company's IT. He felt his in-house team wasn't getting the best results. They had a problem with IT delivery.

The first question I asked was, "How many end users do you have? How many staff members use a computer, a tablet, or a smartphone for work?"

He replied, "I don't know, maybe fifty or seventy-five."

So I asked, "How many people do you have on your IT staff helping to support your infrastructure, your help desk, and all the other parts of IT?"

He told me there were two. One of them was the IT manager. However, it became apparent as we spoke that nobody was actually doing IT management—not the CFO, not the president, not even the IT manager. Why not? None of them really knew how to manage IT. The guy whose title was IT manager didn't know how to integrate management and planning into his scope of work.

So I said, "Well, let's do some math here. One of your

IT people, the one with the manager title, is probably making in the high five figures or maybe $100,000, and the other is probably closer to around $60,000. If you add in the extra staffing costs of hiring, benefits, and taxes, you're paying another 20% to 30% on top of that. So your monthly costs are probably in the $18,000 range."

He said, "Yeah, and as a matter of fact, we're really upset because we feel like we're being held hostage by the IT manager."

A common situation, as we've already seen. So I said, "Given the size of your company and your IT needs, you can readily outsource the whole thing. You'd eliminate the issues we've talked about and save better than 50% in cost at the same time. You'd be paying $6,000 to $8,000 a month."

As it turned out, that's just what they did. They're getting far better results today and saving about $10,000 a month by outsourcing.

Aligning Resources With Goals

I was called in by a company that had a fairly extensive IT department. They had help-desk people, an IT director, and staff assigned to all areas of information technology. They had about three hundred end users. They also had one of those situations where IT problems were an excuse for staff not to work. It wasn't that management wasn't trying. The problem was that they didn't know how to bring IT in line with their goals.

The first thing we did as consultants was to draw up an IT plan. We engaged them in discussion: What are your goals? Where are you trying to get to? They needed to align their resources with a strategy. We helped them create a road map of costs from an IT perspective.

What we did was put in place weekly company leadership meetings. They weren't doing this before. We developed a full spectrum of best practices in order to standardize their IT. We helped them get to the root causes of their IT problems and implemented a brand new IT system from soup to nuts, the help desk to security.

We also implemented a wide range of service levels so that they would be able to understand and deal with difficulties if they arose. We showed them how to plan instead of react. As consultants we provided them with full IT project management. In the process, we were able to lower the cost of their overall IT investment. In the end, they obtained better results than they'd ever thought possible.

I was consulted by a heating company that did not have an internal IT department. They'd had their IT set up by an outsourcer with whom they'd lost confidence, and now nobody was responsible for their IT.

I spoke with them about their issues and came to the conclusion that we'd need to completely evaluate and do an assessment and health check of their entire IT system. Next we assigned a member of my team to act as their fractional CIO. In consultation with the company management, this fractional CIO began drawing up plans to take the firm's information technology from where it was to where it needed to be. We had to understand their business from the inside out in order to be able to forecast and execute their technology.

We sent out a network administrator to document every process to better understand and systematize the working mechanics of their business. We implemented backup and disaster-recovery programs, which they hadn't had before. We provided a help desk to ensure that when they call for troubleshooting, a member of my team would start to work on their problem within two minutes, instead of two days as they'd experienced with their previous outsourcer.

We implemented systems management and best practices

to deliver up time and productivity. We instituted short but frequent planning sessions so they'd understand what needs to be done and when, both from a technical and business perspective. Our process, which is still ongoing, involves a weekly conference call between our IT team and their operations person and general manager. This establishes ongoing accountability and responsibility for IT.

A member of our team leads the meetings and tracks the action items to make sure that nothing holds the company back, nothing goes unfixed or creates delays, all questions are answered. These meetings are important because we need to be constantly gathering facts on the ground. We need to know if something isn't working so that we can deal with it before it escalates. If we have to buy equipment or make system improvements, we want to get started as soon as possible.

Getting Up to Speed

What's curious is that sometimes when we implement an IT assessment process, an organization will push back. Management may be somewhat uncomfortable because they're not used to being accountable for IT.

I try to help them understand that efficient management

of IT will positively impact productivity throughout their organization. For most business professionals, it's a completely new perspective on technology.

Gradually they begin to understand how much they need to get up to speed, whether their IT is in-house or outsourced. As consultants, we can implement best practices, but we need company managers to commit to strategic planning and budgeting. If the client doesn't approve the budget for a project, they simply can't go forward with that portion of their IT plan.

When it comes to outsourcing, accountability is a two-way street. Responsibility is shared by both the company and the outsourcer. But, as already noted, the buck stops with company management. There's no other way to make it work.

When you *Do IT Right*, whether in-house, outsourced, or hybrid, company end users are productive, wait times are next to zero, new processes and business strategy support growth, and business has the edge in a competitive market.

Now that you know your options, let's take a closer look at how IT maximizes efficiency, adds value, and increases competitive advantage.

6

The IT Solution

If we think of strategic IT as the top floor of a ten-story building, you don't want to be on the ground floor. You don't want to be running for the elevator or jockeying just to get on. You want to feel secure and on the rise with an effective information technology plan and strategy. You want your information technology integrated, transparent, and central to your overall business plan. You want to be ascending past your competition on the lower floors as you optimize your way to the top.

From where I stand as a business person and IT consultant, I see that many executives haven't yet stepped onto the elevator. Sure they want to turbo-charge their business. Doesn't everyone? But when it comes to IT, they're down in the lobby at the concession buying another cup of coffee.

End the Chaos

As an outsourcer, I know I have to prove my value to my customers every day. I need to be continually effective in optimizing my clients' information technology and IT management. An employer will fire a consultant a lot more quickly than he or she will fire an employee.

Clients frequently ask me how much they should be spending on IT.

I have one client who invests millions of dollars a year in custom software development. It gives his company a giant competitive advantage. They're a trucking company that wants to know exactly what they're doing. They want to know precisely where their drivers are. They want to know the best routes, and they want the ability to adjust quickly to traffic, weather, and other factors. Customization gives them the competitive edge. Meanwhile, their competitors are buying off-the-shelf software that provides no clear advantage.

How good do you want to be? How much do you think Amazon spends on their technology? Can you compare what Amazon spends to the guy down the street?

Of course, businesses want to be practical and contain costs as much as possible, especially when starting out. So how much should your business spend on IT?

The fact is that many companies are spending more, not less, than they need to for IT. And they're not getting the best possible results. They are operating far below the level of optimization. They're running redundant applications, their infrastructure isn't optimized, capacity is excessive, and energy is wasted.

Companies want and need sustainable value for their investment. Note that "investment" is the most appropriate word when it comes to IT, far better than "cost" or "spending." Decision-making in the twenty-first century should be enabled by data. IT should be aligned with a company's goals and advance its vision and objectives.

When it comes to business planning and IT strategy, most managers aren't even close. They are only talking about what's broken today. They are so intimidated by the technical aspects of IT that they prefer to ignore it or blindly consider IT "handled." They pass the responsibility for their company's IT to the technical experts. They hire an individual or a tech team or a consultant and assume it will all be dealt with. And when things don't quite work out, they believe they know who to blame.

Unfortunately, they're missing the boat on IT. They don't recognize the opportunities inherent in technology. From the start, they don't know who to hire or how to adequately define expectations. They fail to put standard businesses practices in place to manage their company's IT. They aren't planning ahead, and what makes matters worse, their IT people aren't planning either. As the old saying goes, "It takes two to tango."

Entrepreneurs have great business acumen; they are natural risk takers. But when it comes to IT, they stumble. When problems arise, they react by seeking the quickest way out of the chaos. That's usually when I get a call. It's an SOS.

My goal in my work and throughout this book is to end the IT chaos. Every company needs to be more proactive and less reactive with their IT.

Your IT Environment

When I get that call for a consultation, the proverbial mess has already hit the fan. The company desperately needs someone to come in and clean house.

I've consulted with companies that were way overspending on their IT payroll. We've been able to help cut that cost in half. We evaluate in-house staff positions to see if any techs are incorrectly placed in the wrong jobs. Each of those positions has to be accountable. If there are no metrics to start with, we work at building them into the IT management and planning structure.

In getting to the root causes of IT inefficiencies in an organization, my staff and I document all of a client's technology, and input that information into a database. We have technicians looking at workflows, while others are setting up systems administration and network administration. We have an architect looking for ways to maximize efficiencies.

What we do is plan the client's entire IT environment. It's what every company needs to do. Deficiencies slow down growth. IT done right makes the difference between a business that is working effectively and one that is slowed down by having to call the help desk every time there's a problem, not to mention never being able to gain a competitive advantage.

One small company with a single in-house IT specialist was in the dark about how to improve their processes. Their IT guy was basically good at what he did, but he was stretched too far. It didn't take long to figure out the areas in which his skills were best suited. We recommended they hire a second person for a help desk and other responsibilities. In this case they had to increase their payroll spending, but the efficiencies gained were well worth the additional investment.

Investments in technology need to be well thought out. This is why I stress sound management principles that include measurable service levels and metrics. Effective business planning requires ongoing evaluation of IT. You can't just manage based on current IT being "busy."

As Peter Drucker, the founder of modern management, said, "What is measured improves," and leadership is "defined by results."

IT Maximizes Value

When IT correctly meets an organization's needs, it adds tangible value. It doesn't just support the enterprise; it integrates many different parts into a working whole. Value derives from maximizing investment.

Part of the way to get maximum value from your IT is to eliminate unnecessary complexities. Some IT systems at older companies have layers of complexity built one atop of the other. When we're asked to come in as consultants, we have to go digging deep into systems and processes.

As we've seen in this book, it isn't just software and hardware, systems and networks, that add complexity, but people as well. Inefficient placement of staff, maintenance that is ignored, tasks that go unaccounted for, poor management or no management, uninformed decision-making and inadequate planning—all add to complexity.

The alternative is to track data and benchmarks at the management level, make timely upgrades, see to ongoing maintenance, and plan for growth. Efficient IT yields increased value across the board. Long-term planning yields flexibility. Instead of running to catch up, the company is planning ahead and making critical decisions before facts on the ground push their hand. Annual budgets should account for strategic investment in information technology.

As described in Chapter 4, companies need to forecast expenditures for IT growth three to five years out. This is how funding is aligned with strategy. Service levels are measured, and projects are tracked. Decisions stem from concrete data and objectives.

Companies are always looking toward growth and seeking to expand their capabilities. IT alignment with growth exists along a continuum from preventive maintenance to upgrades to new enabling technologies. When IT is maximized and integrated, it provides a business with the agility to adapt to an evolving marketplace and industry trends.

Strategic IT drives business value. Therefore, the architecture of a company's IT should reflect goals, capabilities, and investment needs. A bus company that wants to expand its service area must plan an appropriate IT road map to reach that goal. A distribution company preparing to market a new product can't be guessing about IT capability. When it comes to growth, IT can't be an afterthought. It should be integral to the process.

Disruptive Technology

A common misconception about information technology is that IT is basically business support, and nothing more.

I hope this book has shown you that IT is not merely a tool, an add-on, or an afterthought. Business leaders are coming to realize that IT is increasingly the lifeblood of an organization. It's an information distribution system that nourishes every cell of the corporate body. In this analogy, IT security systems are like antibodies traveling along information arteries to reach every corner of an organization, protecting against viruses and hacks.

More than ever, IT is driving business innovation and driving down costs. In these changing times, IT even extends past innovation to disruption. IT is hardly a tool; it's a serious industry disrupter.

Case in point: Uber.

As a technology-driven innovation on traditional taxi service, Uber has transformed the urban transportation landscape. Taxi service is an $11 billion industry. But as anyone who's ever waited in the rain to flag down a cab knows, an available taxi just isn't there when you need it. Enter Uber and Lyft with connected models that tap into handheld technologies with dynamic service and pricing based on supply and demand. It stands to reason that mobility should be accessible by mobile apps.

In *Do IT Right* we've seen how companies with field operations, such as mechanical services, upgrade their systems to mobile platforms. They want to optimize their business model and speed service from order to dispatch to technicians in the field. Interconnectivity is their key to maximizing IT value to best the competition.

Consider a product such as Amazon's Kindle reader. I've mentioned Amazon several times in this book because as a company they epitomize strategic investment in IT.

Amazon's founder Jeff Bezos wasn't content to sit back selling books online. He expanded inventory across the board to retail everything from food to footwear. Amazon connects customers to other retailers while collecting data and commissions on sales. By harnessing disruptive technology, the Web-based company has positioned itself at the crossroads of retail and payment systems, entertainment studios and original content, delivery drones and Web services. Amazon bundled high-speed Internet into its Kindle to deliver books digitally and instantaneously, directly to the customer's hand.

From mainframe to PC to Cloud-based computing, every innovation in information technology has proven disruptive to business as usual. Which is why I tell my customers, "If you want to grow and you want to compete at the top, business as usual just isn't good enough."

When Groupon set out to market daily deals in the global marketplace, it needed business-application software to conduct business from regional offices across four continents. They considered the traditional model of hosting applications on-site in their own data centers, but found it way too complicated for their needs. Instead they opted for Web-based Cloud applications, called "software as a service," or SaaS, which could be easily scaled to their rapidly growing customer base. They didn't need to build and maintain their own IT infrastructure.

Not every enterprise would make the same decision. Needs vary from business to business. Factors of size, location, scale, and compliance are all variables. Cloud-based SaaS would not be the best option for organizations that need to comply with privacy laws or other regulations that don't permit outside hosting. When applications are critical to an enterprise, a company would choose to contain risk by keeping their IT exclusively in-house. For a large company with an established on-site data center, it's probably cost-effective to continue hosting new business applications themselves. However, a company that has maxed out its data storage capacity may find it convenient to move some business applications to the Cloud.

The point is to maximize IT efficiency and build it into planning and management. Companies can't necessarily see the next new disruptive technology on the horizon, but by continually upgrading their systems, they maintain flexibility. They are always positioned to compete.

Marketing underwent a revolution with the introduction of Internet-friendly iPhones and Android devices. It became possible for advertisers to reach customers anytime, anyplace, and to keep their messages timely, immediate, relevant, and fun. Marketing and advertising made the leap from newspaper, radio, and TV to search engines, email, social networks, newsfeeds, and blogs.

In these competitive times, every business with something to sell or services to offer has a website, a Facebook page, a blog, Snapchat, Periscope, and a Twitter account. Every digital venue has its own disruptive influence. Yelp provides space for businesses to profile themselves and share information, and for visitors to rate businesses.

As a business-related networking site, LinkedIn connects individuals and companies through profiles and company pages where products and services are promoted. Google+ is an integrated platform for local-based marketing and search services with extensive reach. The mobile app Instagram is a platform for brand marketing and interaction between businesses and consumers.

No business wants to be behind the curve of information technology. Disruptive technologies continually create new markets and new value. In the course of human history, nothing has been more disruptive to the status quo than technology. Whether it was the disruptive shift from stone tools to metal, or telephones to handheld computers, we embraced the new or were left behind.

It's Not About the Computer

Many times throughout this book, I've said IT isn't about the computer. Instead, IT is about the following:

- Communication
- Information flow
- Connectivity
- Business management
- People
- Getting results
- Security
- Innovation
- Growing a business
- Strategic investment
- Getting ahead of the curve
- Besting the competition
- Creative disruption
- Reducing risk
- Culture
- And so much more...

Another way of expressing this concept is to say, "Today everything is a computer." Information technology is everywhere and part of everything, especially in business. IT fuels our economy, our work and leisure time, and our vision for the future.

If you're a business professional and you've read through this book, you're now more informed about IT than the vast majority of your peers and, of course, your competition. You've come to see how vital IT is for strategizing and business planning. You've gained insight into how to *think* about IT.

Any business owner who wants her company to thrive, any executive who wants to earn his keep, needs to embrace information technology. If your company's IT isn't delivering on your expectations, then you need to change your approach.

When you *Do IT Right*, you'll get excellent return on investment. When you apply best business practices, sound management principles, measurable metrics, and service levels to IT, you will best your competition. When you know how to assemble an IT team and put the right people in place, or outsource to qualified IT consultants, you'll be thinking like an IT-savvy CEO.

IT doesn't deserve the bad rap it gets. It isn't a necessary evil. You've seen how misinformation about IT in the business world stems from poor management and insecurity. But organizations are turning their IT problems around. They are learning to take IT to new levels of efficiency for their companies, and they are reaping the rewards.

Managers are learning to manage their company's IT with the kind of reporting and benchmarking they use for every other section of their business. They budget and plan in advance for the most effective IT framework. They consult with in-house teams or hire consultants with whom they can strategize.

Smart business leaders are learning how to leverage IT for sustainable growth. As we've seen, innovation in business today hinges on technology. We can't just get IT up and running and leave it in place until the battery runs down. IT is not the RonCo 4000 Rotisserie oven; we can't "set it and forget it." We need to continually assess, maintain, and upgrade systems. Thinking like a CIO means leveraging emerging technologies.

It's Your Turn to *Do IT Right*

Today we are at a crossroads where data, social networking, mobility, and Cloud computing are converging. New business models are emerging. As we've seen with software as a service, companies no longer have to build their own IT infrastructure. There's more flexibility than ever before in how IT is delivered. Our IT-driven marketplace is rapidly changing.

Businesses are optimizing IT and reducing complexity

at the same time. The evolution of IT is always toward greater ease of information flow and data accessibility. The goal of IT and of companies themselves is to reduce any friction that slows business down.

Day-to-day business operations are more entwined with IT today than ever before. From marketing to revenue streams, IT is the engine that drives growth. No one who wants to get ahead in business today can take IT for granted. Our smartest business leaders are maximizing the alliance of information technology and industry.

More than ever, corporate performance hinges on optimizing IT. Software is changing, and business applications are getting smarter. Cloud computing is increasingly a driver of innovation.

When I say, "Everything is a computer," it's another way of saying, "Everything is connected," which leads us to the emerging new world of the "Internet of Things."

Imagine a world in which everyday objects, from your car to your home, your refrigerator to your water heater, are as connected to the data stream as your smartphone. We enter a world of smart technologies in which manufacturers and retailers can adjust product and supply based on long-range weather patterns. The supply chain is equipped with built-in digital controls. Energy is managed through a smart grid.

Individual businesses will ride that data stream or be left scratching their heads. There will be no middle ground and nowhere to shift the blame.

We are entering a world of "*Do IT Right* or get out of the game." As I've said, and as every savvy business leader knows, effective IT management is where the rubber hits the road. Our cars will soon be automated, but business management will not. Managers will have better choices and more sophisticated tools, but they'll still be making the decisions.

When you synchronize IT with your overall business strategy, you'll achieve adaptability in real time. When your company's goals and course of growth are aligned with IT, you'll be adaptive to change. You'll be positioned to embrace disruptive technologies for competitive advantage.

I hope that by reading this book you've learned how to *think* effectively about IT. If you've learned how to maximize IT to grow your business and earn your market share, then I've done my job. Now it's your turn to *Do IT Right*.

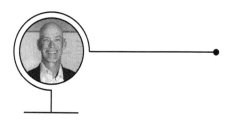

About the Author

MARTY KAUFMAN is Founder and President of Accent Computer Solutions, Inc., a Southern California-based innovator in IT thinking. Marty has spent his entire career researching and implementing Information Technology strategies and processes to help executives get better business results from their IT. He lives with his family in Southern California.

Made in the USA
San Bernardino, CA
26 June 2017